To Trevor
I Hope you enjoy my
Book
Chrissie
x

A Look Inside the Therapy Room

A Look Inside the Therapy Room

ISBN: 978-1-8384749-7-3

First published in Great Britain
in 2023 through Amazon self-publishing
service Kindle Direct Publishing

Produced in the UK by The Book Writers' Resource
www.tbwr.co.uk

Declaration

The experiences shared in this book are real life accounts. Names and personal details have been changed to protect identities and maintain confidentiality.

Permission has been granted by clients whose stories are featured in this book.

I would like to say a massive thank you to everyone who has allowed me to share their experiences.

Why I Wrote this Book

HAVE YOU EVER WONDERED WHAT happens in the therapy room? This book, *A Look Inside the Therapy Room,* aims to answer commonly asked questions by clients and people looking for therapy. My aim is to dismiss your fears and taboos of what happens in the therapy.

As a private therapist, I am only going to meet a percentage of the people I can support. Writing this book gives me the opportunity to reach out to many more—most of whom I may never meet face-to-face—so I can provide you with an insight into the world of therapy from my perspective and share a little about me.

I will be giving answers to questions you may have if you are looking for books on therapy or considering entering therapy yourself.

I never thought I would ever write a book, always thinking it was something other people do, but then I thought, 'why not share my story and experiences if it helps somebody else?'

What you will gain from reading my book.

An insider's view of what happens in therapy.

Until you take time to get to know other people you never really know what they have to offer and what you can learn from them and their life experiences. Getting to know "you" is an amazing part of the work I do.

There may be something you want to read in this book and there maybe something you need to read but haven't yet realised it.

You may get the answers you are looking for, but be prepared to be left with questions you want answering too. That's the beauty of knowledge, we usually want more.

I have included 'Pause for Thought' pages. These start with prompt questions at the end of some chapters for you to reflect on your thoughts, feelings and emotions, about what you have just read, your own experiences, or space just to make notes.

Chrissie

www.counsellingwithchrissie.co.uk
chrissiehenson@hotmail.com

Contents

A Look Inside the Therapy Room

Chrissie Henson
Therapist

Prologue

My Story

I WAS BORN IN THE early 70s and let's just say life decided to challenge me from the very start. The youngest of five children and a twin, my birth was anything from straight-forward. I was born six weeks premature, as my twin was delivered, I was somehow pushed upwards and my foot became trapped in my mum's ribcage, with no time for a C-section, I was pulled out with suckers and born medically dead! After being resuscitated, it was apparent I had been starved of oxygen and had to go to the ICU. Before they could transfer me I died another eight times, due to infantile convulsions, meaning that I had technically died nine times in my first day of my life. I remained in hospital for the first two months before going home on Christmas Eve. I was only expected to reach my first birthday.

The term used back then was 'a poor start in life', and it was during a hospital visit 18 months later where my dad overheard a doctor telling a group of student doctors about the child with cerebral palsy. This child was me, and this is how we found out and this is how we found out the name of my disability.

To help me get the level of physiotherapy I required, I was sent to a special needs school at just 2.5-years-old—far too young in my opinion. How do you form positive attachments with your mum and dad if you are at school all day? But those kind of things were not thought about in those days.

I stayed in special needs education until I was nine—I loved it! Small classes with teachers who saw what I loved—singing and maths—and encouraged me to do well in both. Although, I did have daily arguments with the school physio about not doing my exercises; taking me swimming every Friday was a headache for them as I did everything in my power not to get in that pool.

It was then decided that I was being 'held back' and would do better in a mainstream junior school—not that anybody had ever asked me. I was merely told before being taken to see my sister's school which I started the following year.

Whilst my strength of character held me in good stead for mainstream schooling, the number of children, the hustle and bustle, the people making fun of my disability, and losing my identity as I became the 'twin sister', NOT Chrissie, were some of the things I was not prepared for.

If having my hair pulled and being deliberately pushed over for two years wasn't bad enough for me to deal with, at home my dad had suffered a nervous breakdown and spent months in bed. I remember going to cuddle him thinking it would make him better, like his cuddles with me always made me feel better, but sadly this was not the case.

Who could I tell about the bullying, Mum had her hands full and Dad was too poorly.

Things improved when I moved to senior school after I met a nice group of friends. There were times when other kids tried to make fun of me but nothing went on for too long, having a big sister in the school gave me protection.

On leaving school I decided I wanted to work with children. The careers officer gave the usual advice for people with a disability, 'get a job in a bank' —not helpful. I went to college for a year to gain a BTEC qualification in care. This was supposed to lead me into my Nursery Nursing course, but the tutors decided I wasn't capable of working with children. They wouldn't allow me to enroll on the course. I still remember that day; the 'nice' tutor holding my hand and asking me what I was going to do instead now no one would give me a job working with children.

I left college and after numerous knock backs and getting to know the 'Oh my god, you're disabled,' look on the faces of the interviewers, I got a job, and guess what? It was working with children.

I would love to say this is my happily ever after, but sadly this was where I experienced my first taste of discrimination in the workplace. A member of staff 20 years my senior mimicked my voice in a negative way. After it was reported and 'dealt with' (nothing happened to him), the majority of the other staff then stopped speaking to me because I had reported their friend.

It was during this time I also experienced my first bereavement, my best friend from when we were five, passed away suddenly from her disability at just 21. Not only was I dealing with losing my best friend, I also had fears that I would die early from my disability. The stress of both situations resulted in me experiencing therapy for the first time.

I eventually left that job, and had many years in different roles, some I loved, others just paid the bills.

It wasn't until 2011 when I experienced discrimination at work again for my speech. This time it was due to team members thinking my project management work was easier or better than the work they did—the 'grass must be greener' syndrome—and a manager who let the team dictate to him what work I should do. He attempted to move me to a telephone role, but this time I knew my rights. I had been employed with the understanding that I had speech difficulties and that phone duties were very limited. I went to HR and a new 'less demanding' role was created, but it was nothing like the project management role I had loved doing.

The treatment from the team members and manager, along with issues in my private life led me to feel isolated, rejected and without purpose resulting in suicidal thoughts. With lots of therapy and three months off work, I recovered and started to rebuild my life. I got my dog, Angel, for company during this time.

I was made redundant 18 months later, it was at that point I decided I was going to become a therapist.

Again, I would love to say this was a turning point in my life but again, I experienced discrimination. It happened when a placement supervisor stated that I should work with animals instead of people, that my disability would be too much for the clients to handle, and would stop them focusing on their issues. Again, I knew my rights, and took this to management. She left her post before being asked to leave.

With all the things I have experienced, I feel I have been training to be a therapist my whole life. Happily, it enables me to support others.

Since starting my private practice, I haven't experienced any other issues of discrimination and really love working with the people I meet. I have a fantastic, supportive supervisor, who encourages me to be the therapist I want to be.

Sadly my dad never got to see me start my own business or write this book as he passed away from cancer in 2007, but I know how proud of me he would be.

Continue reading to see how I work as a therapist, and how I have supported so many amazing people over the last six years.

Read a little more about me in the 'About the Author' chapter later in the book.

A LOOK INSIDE THE THERAPY ROOM

Pause for Thought

Do you relate to my story?
How has reading it left you feeling?

Your notes:

Your notes:

1

Does Therapy Work for Everyone?

What is therapy?

THERAPY IS REGULAR TIME WITH a qualified and experienced professional that aims to give you space to identify your thoughts, feelings and emotions, to explore why they are causing you distress and what you can do to improve your life. It is about growing your confidence and self-esteem, so you feel empowered to make changes and have healthier relationships with yourself and others.

Does therapy work for everyone? Absolutely not. Therapy is hard. Unless you are willing to work and examine yourself inside and out. Check your expectations are realistic and identify what triggers behaviour, or you will make the same mistakes over and over. Therapy isn't just about what happens in the sessions, it's a process. Sometimes it can take months, depending on how deep you have buried your issues and how much work you are willing to put in.

You need to be there for you, not because your mum, dad, boyfriend, wife, friend etc., thinks you need therapy or they have had therapy and it worked for them. Or because they are in therapy and you thought you should see what it is like, or they are paying for your sessions. I have seen it all and many of these clients don't come back for more than two sessions—they don't have anything to work on or they are not there for themselves. It could be they are simply not ready to do the work needed to change or just don't really want to be in therapy.

Therapy is a big investment physically, mentally and emotionally. If you are going to have therapy, please do it for yourself.

I am not what happened to me, I am what I choose to become.
Carl Jung.

Pause for Thought

Have you been to therapy before?
What did you find helpful?
What didn't work for you and why?

Your notes:

Your notes:

2

Different Kinds of Therapy

What is the difference between private therapy, a self help book/course or NHS therapy?

SOMETIMES WHEN WE TRY AND work on our issues alone, we only have our own answers to resolve the problem. Whilst this works for many, for some people, having another person's input can help—a problem shared and all that. This could be a family member or trusted friend but they will also have their opinion on what you could/should do and want to make you feel 'better', so may just tell you what to do. It's often easier to see how others can resolve their problems as we are not feeling the emotions you have alongside the problem.

Some people choose to see a therapist instead. As a qualified therapist, you benefit from my knowledge, understanding and tools. My years of experience enables me to ask appropriate questions while listening for both what is and isn't being said. I hear what you may not—the meaning behind the words. Having a conversation opens up new thoughts and generates new ideas and ways of thinking. Sometimes it's about being told you are believed, important and worthy, and being supported on a regular basis.

Self-help books give you information but don't look at why you have arrived where you are today. You only get your perspective or interpretation on what you are reading. This can work short term, but the books are not about you as an individual or your life experiences. They don't know the real you.

NHS talking therapies are mainly offered to those experiencing depression or anxiety and is treated with Cognitive Behavioural Therapy (CBT).

Sessions can be done in a workbook, online, or by phone. A few people will get have face-to-face sessions with a therapist. You are given an initial telephone assessment to discover which service you are suitable for, before being placed on a waiting list or given a workbook.

People diagnosed with mental health conditions like bipolar get access to a psychologist.

- I have worked with clients whilst they were waiting to access this service, for some it took 18 months or longer!

While NHS services can benefit you and are free, you may wait months before getting the help you want and need. The NHS define CBT as:

> [a] talking therapy that can help you manage your problems by changing the way you think

and behave. It's most commonly used to treat anxiety and depression, but can be useful for other mental and physical health problems. www.nhs.uk*

* NHS UK, available at: https://www.nhs.uk/mental-health/talking-therapies-medicine-treatments/talking-therapies-and-counselling/cognitive-behavioural-therapy-cbt/overview/

Pause for Thought

What would you talk about in therapy?
What would you want to achieve?

Your notes:

Your notes:

My Problem Is...

How do you work with this?

The real answer is: I work with you,
or rather, we work together.

YOU SET THE AGENDA, AFTER all, it's your time and you know what's affecting you in this moment.

To help you, I will use open questions which encourage you to think deeper and explore other perspectives. Being questioned can feel difficult to begin with but it is essential to understand yourself better and therefore become more empowered.

While I'm carefully listening to you, I am also looking for what isn't being said, the thoughts and feelings behind your words, your body language, your tone of voice and the words you are using. This helps us to understand the deeper meanings and give you the right tools to help you.

This is where we go deeper, sometimes needing to look at your past to see where your thoughts, beliefs, and learned behaviours come from. Are they truly yours? Or have they been passed down to you from parents, carers, teachers, and other influential people in your childhood?

I don't 'treat' anyone, my role is to provide you a safe space where you can explore your issues.

I am a person-centred therapist. This means I put you at the centre of your therapy. You choose what we talk about each session and where you want the therapy to go.

Angelica Bottaro* discusses that person-centred therapy (Rogerian therapy) was developed in the 1940s by humanist

---

* Angelica Bottaro, verywellhealth.com available at: https://www.verywellhealth.com/person-centered-therapy-5218356

psychologist Carl Rogers. She explains that the therapy focusses on the client rather than the mental health professional and that the client is then empowered to take control of the therapeutic process. It was believed by Rogers that every person, regardless of mental health, is capable of reaching their full potential.

Bottaro states that Rogerian therapy practice steers away from the idea that humans are flawed, requiring treatment for their behavioural issues. It provides clients with the tools and resources they require to achieve positive change in their lives through understanding themselves.

Within my work I also use CBT techniques and creative tasks if clients wish to use them.

How can you work with me?

You can choose one of my courses that resonates with you; you can work alone, or we can work together with therapy sessions.

You can attend therapy sessions online using my online therapy room.

You can come for face-to-face therapy in my room.

All information can be found at:

www.counsellingwithchrissie.co.uk

What can you say in the session?

It is your time. Say what is on your mind the most, say what you want to change, say what is causing you physical and emotional pain.

You can also bring your successes and what has made you happier.

Be the real you and we can start from there.

4

Therapy with a Difference

What makes you different? Or better than other therapists

ME; MY LIFE EXPERIENCES; MY outlook; my viewpoints; all make me the therapist I am and is what allows me to work with you in my unique way. That's not to say I'm right for everyone—only you can decide that—but most people know this from our initial contact or first session.

In my opinion, I'm no better than any other therapists. Nor are they any better than me. We are all different, and it is my uniqueness that makes me the therapist I am. My background of living with cerebral palsy, the challenges throughout my life, discrimination, bullying, and the determination it has taken to still be me and run my own business, all contribute to my uniqueness.

Everyone who enters therapy training is there for their own reason. I've always wanted to be able to support people through their dark times, for them to have someone who wants to be there for them. To listen and hear them, truly hear them, and sit for as many sessions as it takes until they find the solutions they need to be happier. To choose different paths or even help them to learn to live with what they can't change.

5

Working with Your Issues

WHAT ISSUES DO YOU WORK WITH? WHAT IS YOUR AREA OF EXPERTISE?

BELOW ARE SOME OF THE areas I work with, for a full list please visit my website: counsellingwithchrissie.co.uk

Young adults / students

*Life changes.
*Stresses of college / university life.
*Peer pressure / problems.
*Challenges of living away from home.
*Relationship difficulties.
*Identifying who you are as an adult.
*Work demands.
*Body issues and eating disorders.

Confidence or low self esteem

*Can lead to depression.
*Self-isolation.
*Little / no interest in life.
*Suicidal thoughts.

*Work issues.
*Family difficulties.
*Past experiences creating today's problems.

See my Ladder of Change course available at: bitesizetherapy.bigcartel.com

- Is there an area in your life you are wanting to change? This helpful tool can guide you through the process.

Disability – visible and non-visible

*Social exclusion.
*Work issues, finding / keeping work.
*Benefit worries.
*Disability / illness concerns / fears.
*Family difficulties.
*Problems / fears socialising.
*Medical appointments concerns.
*Not being heard.
*Needs overlooked because disability is non-visible.

Relationship issues

*Conflict.
*Pleasing others.
*Not feeling valued or heard.
*Feeling trapped.
*Work issues.
*Family difficulties.
*Past relationships creating today's problems.

See my "Who you Attract" course available in the bite size therapy section of my website:

www.counsellingwithchrissie.co.uk
bitesizetherapy.bigcartel.com*

Emotionally absent parent

*Attachment issues.
*Narcissistic or critical parenting.
*Looking for substitute parents in adult relationships.
*Low self-esteem.
*Low resilience.

---

* An in depth look at the relationships you are attracting and how you can change them.

LGBTQ

*Identifying which community you belong to.
*Stigma.
*Fears of telling family and friends.
*Learning to be the real you.
*Accepting who you are.
*Living without guilt / shame.
Anxiety and depression.
*Identifying fears.
*What you are avoiding.
*Panic attacks.
*Self-esteem issues.
*Low mood.
*Triggers.
*Managing stress levels.

See my CBT course available at:

bitesizetherapy.bigcartel.com

- Gain a basic knowledge of how to use Cognitive behavioural Therapy to help retrain your negative thoughts.

Self-Harm

*Why you think you deserve to be hurt.
*Triggers.
*Your first aid kit.
*Letter to self.
*Changing thought patterns.
*Find other ways to release stress.
*Abuse.
*Past or present physical abuse.
*Sexual abuse.
*Emotional abuse.
*Psychological abuse or gas lighting.
*Financial abuse.
*Domestic violence.
*Self-neglect.

6 Starting Therapy

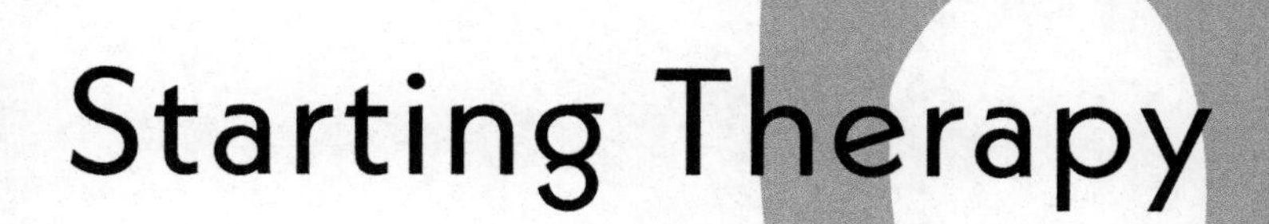

What is my role inbetween our sessions?

SOMETHING I SHARE WITH MY clients before we start working together is to write down why they are coming for therapy, what they hope to change, "my reasons for doing this are..." etc.

This is so we have something to refer back to, to help us stay on track. It's very easy once you are in therapy to slip into talking about what's happened that week; whilst this is important, it's also important to remember what you came for in the beginning and work on that. It's a very powerful 'tool' to go back to during—and at the end of—therapy to see what has changed and see how far you have come.

During the sessions you can do as much or as little as you want to. Some people just come, let out what they are holding and then nothing until their next session. Whilst this is their choice, the progress can be very slow and it takes longer to achieve their goals. Others ask for homework, writing what they liked and disliked about the sessions, what was helpful or unhelpful, then using the tools/new knowledge from the sessions. These clients see change a lot quicker and have longer periods between sessions or returning to therapy. Some never need to return to therapy as they have found answers that work for them.

I feel honoured months later when they contact me saying how much I have changed their lives, knowing that they really did all the hard work.

Starting therapy questions

What brought you to therapy and why now?

a) Feelings
b) thoughts
c) current problems.

How will you know when you've achieved what you came for?

a) What will it look like?
b) What will it feel like?

How much of what you want to achieve is within your power?

How willing are you to change?

Score 1–10

a) How would you score your current life?
b) How much of a negative effect has the problem had on your life?
c) How important is it for you to feel better?

d) How willing are you to make getting better a priority in your life?

7 The Sessions

What happens in the sessions? How many can I have?

Every session along with every client is different.

THE FIRST SESSION USUALLY STARTS with us agreeing a contract of how we wish to work together—a discussion about confidentiality, how we will work together, boundaries and data protection. All of which will be available before you start your first session*. You have the rest of the session explaining why you are there and what you want from therapy.

The following sessions are led by you; what

---

* Information on how I store your information can be found on my website: www.counsellingwithchrissie.co.uk

you want to talk about; going over anything you have worked on or experienced during the week, good and bad. Exploring the thoughts and feelings attached to your problems, sometimes ones you didn't realise you had.

Every client will use their time differently, talking, crying, doing nothing but sitting and enjoying the space, engaging in two-way conversations and wanting my input. That's why therapy is so special, there are no rules on what you 'have to do.' it's all about you what you want and need.

Some therapists and clients only work in the session. I will, if clients agree, set homework on occasion, which encourages you to go deeper. It's your choice if you complete it.

Keeping a journal or book of your time in therapy and the homework you do can be helpful in later months or years, as you can use the same techniques for different issues / problems.

You may not leave every session feeling 'better', sometimes what you explore stays with you. Sometimes you will leave with more questions that you need to explore alone. This is normal and is a sign of progress—as much as when you leave feeling happy.

After you leave, I sit and reflect on the session, making notes and think about what went well in the session, what didn't and where you are going. I will also make brief notes for my supervision, where we discuss an overview of how I am working with you (using your first name only), and how I see the sessions moving forward. The supervisor's role is to check I am working ethically within our set guidelines.

Therapy starts on a weekly basis to give you support while you work through where you are and where you want to get to.

When you are happy that you have fully explored your problems and the new techniques are in place, and more importantly working, you may decide to reduce to fortnightly sessions. These are to discuss progress, setbacks and other issues that may be getting in your way of change. Some people end here whilst others then decide to have monthly sessions to check in with me, maintaining our therapeutic relationship.

There is no right or wrong way as it's an individual's choice, which we discuss during your therapy reviews.

The amount of sessions depends on what you are looking for. Short-term therapy concentrates on the issue concerning you most at the time you seek support. Helping you find solutions, setting goals and ways of coping can take up to 12 sessions.

Long-term goes a lot deeper and works on what has created your thoughts and feelings, and the beliefs and behaviours that are causing you distress in the here and now. We then work on changing them to create a healthy relationship with yourself and others, leading to a happier, fuller life. This can take up to 12 months. Some choose long-term therapy because they don't have a support system or have multiple issues, or they just want to continue building on what they have gained already.

Regular reviews are used to discuss progress and where you want your therapy to go and what you feel you have left to work on.

What happens when therapy ends?

How therapy ends can vary.

A planned ending is where we will prepare and discuss the progress you have made and explore the 'tools' and coping techniques you have to use going forward. These techniques will remind you that you are strong enough to make changes in your life and you deserve to be happy.

A sudden ending is where you decide that

the current session will be your last, that you have the 'tools' and coping techniques you need going forward.

Some just don't want that official goodbye, they like the idea I'm there just in case.

In an ideal world the 'tool kit' you leave with should help you with future issues and empower you to self counsel. You may leave therapy ready to face the world, or you may need to test out your new skills and build what you have started in therapy.

Some clients want to maintain the relationship we have built. Bringing new issues when the arise knowing that their background is already known by me, which is easier than starting again with a new therapist.

Changes can happen straight away or continue to happen weeks or even months after therapy ends. It's a never-ending process.

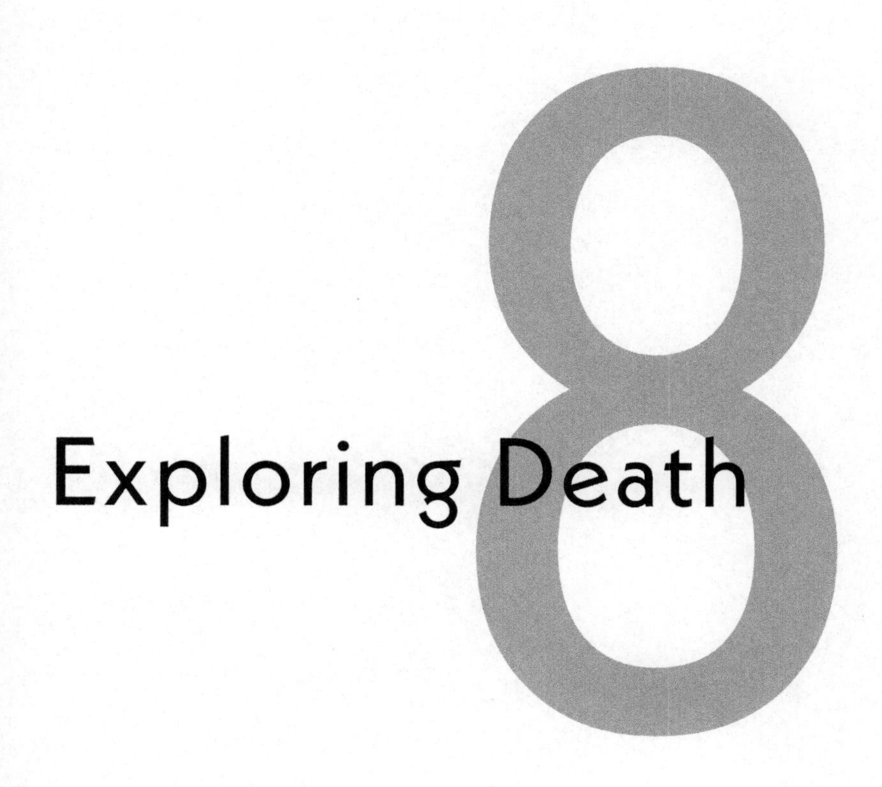

8 Exploring Death

Bereavements, fears of dying and suicide

SUPPORTING CLIENTS THROUGH BEREAVEMENT IS both emotional and rewarding. Bereavement is best described like standing in the sea with your back to the waves. The little waves come and go, you feel they are there but they are ok, not too much. Then every now and again, out of nowhere, the big wave comes and almost knocks you off your feet.

As therapy starts, clients are consumed by their loss and pain, their 'what ifs' and 'whys', often needing to relive the illness and/or ending again. They need to tell someone their story of what happened and have their feelings heard. This can last a couple of sessions or weeks depending on the client and the nature of the passing. As the sessions go by the tears turn to smiles and giggles as they are able to talk about the memories and better times. We often discuss making memory boxes or having pictures or items as memories.

Jane's story

Knowing somebody you love is going to die is possibly one of the hardest things you will ever experience in your life.

Jane, 29, came for therapy after discovering her mum, her only parent, had months to live. Both of them were the only children, so they only had each other in terms of family.

Jane's mum had been diagnosed with a condition that was slowly weakening her heart in its ability to work. She was becoming weaker day by day.

Jane used her time in therapy to explore her feelings and emotions, knowing her mum was going to die. There were lots of tears; unanswered questions on why nobody could make her mum better; feelings of uselessness at not being able to do anything to stop her mum from dying and fears of how she was going to cope without her.

We used our time to explore how she wanted to spend their last weeks together; how she wanted to say goodbye to her mum; how she wanted her funeral to be and how she wanted to remember her mum. Jane made a memory box of her favourite things.

After her mum's passing, Jane continued to come for therapy. It took time to work through her initial grief and loss. Her friends were supportive, although some found her grief too hard and stopped contacting her. Some were there at first, but it quickly went back to Jane being alone.

Jane explored her feelings of hurt and anger

on having her only parent taken away so young, and being left alone without family or friends for support.

Therapy continued for a few months, and we worked together to build on what Jane's life was going to look and feel like going forward. Jane started putting plans into place and eventually felt strong enough to end the therapy.

Jane will always miss her mum, but her time in therapy gave her a safe supportive space to explore that feeling of loss and find out who she was going to be moving forward.

Letter from Sarah

One of my bereavement clients.

> *Chrissie came to me when I was at my lowest. My dad had died nine months before and I'd just given birth to my second child. I was struggling with my dad's passing, and I wasn't coping very well.*

Chrissie came to my house to give me one-to-one counselling and it really helped. She not only listened to me pouring my heart out and crying, she taught me how to put everything into perspective. I wasn't being stupid, as I thought I was, it was normal to be thinking and feeling the way I did at the time.

Chrissie gave me advice on how to cope with my loss and not to dwell on it; she taught me it was ok to cry—crying isn't a bad thing.

The first session I had with Chrissie, I couldn't even talk about my dad without crying, but by my third session I could talk and laugh about the funny things my dad said or did without becoming a wreck. I still cry sometimes when I think about him. I think about him every day and it never gets easier, I'm just learning to come to terms with it.

I can't thank Chrissie enough for what she

has done for me. I always thought talking to a stranger about personal feelings would be a very hard thing to do, but it really isn't, if anything it's much easier than talking to someone close to you in case you upset them.

This is the rewarding part—knowing Sarah was in a happier place when we finished therapy.

For many people the fear of death and dying is overwhelming, leaving behind loved ones, or simply not existing anymore is something they just can't face. Having a loved one who has terminal illness can impact them in two ways: their fears of losing them and their fears of acknowledging their own deaths. This happens more as people get older and friends and family members start showing signs of old age, ill health, and pass away.

Suicidal thoughts

What happens if I tell you I want to kill myself?

Have you ever tried telling someone how bad you feel, only to have your feelings 'watered down' or dismissed? Or you get the, "it's not that bad," "things will change," "be better in the morning," comments? What if they are not better in the morning? Or any time of the day for that matter? What if, for you, the thought of this being your life forever suddenly becomes too much to bear and that voice in your head starts asking THAT question? What's the point of living? Who'll miss me or even care if I'm gone? It's so convincing and very real, maybe this time you'll be strong enough to actually do it.

Sound familiar to you? Have you been here? Are you here at this moment?

The question, "what happens if I tell you I want to kill myself?" is something, sadly, that I have explored with clients on a few occasions. Although, in our initial contracts we do talk about what the danger of harming self and other means, and that I would contact your GP or emergency services. For most people it doesn't come to this—it's a cry for help, wanting desperately for someone to see the pain they are in and to recognise that in this moment—they can't see any other option that will stop the pain and change their awful situation.

So, what does happen? We talk about your plan. Have you got one? Where / how will you do it? Have you tried before? Who do you want to find you? Who do you want to have to tell your partner, kids, parents, families, and friends? What's your interpretation of how they will deal with knowing they didn't get the opportunity to help you, knowing that you chose to end your life and leave them behind? Are you hurting or angry that people are not giving you what you need? What would your answers be?

Poem about suicide

Sorry, I was not there

Sorry I don't run every time you call
But when I need somebody,
there's no one there at all.

Sorry I don't jump every time you shout,
But when I need somebody,
There is nobody about.

Sorry I am not enough, when you are feeling fine.
And you can't give your time to me,
When I always give you mine.

Sorry you can't say "hello"
Or just call for a chat,
I guess, I wasn't worth your time,
And I have to live with that.

So, there'll be no final call
Where you can have your say,
'Cos sadly, when you're ready,
I would have passed away.

Chrissie Henson

Sucicide is the biggest killer of under 35s in the UK. Please seek help if you have ever, or are considering, ending your life.

On writing this poem, my intention is not to highlight suicide as an answer, it's more saying that if others reach out, or even *just* be there, or asking someone going though mental health problems how they are.

It's easy to feel there are no other answers when facing a mental health breakdown without the right support. You don't have to be a trained professional to have a conversation, ask someone what help they need, or just sit and listen.

We can all *make* ourselves *busy* but sometimes it's just remembering to reach out and say, "I'm here for you."

Pause for Thought

How are you feeling in the moment?
Have the stories above triggered any issues for you?

Your notes:

Your notes:

9

Disability and Therapy

Counselling with a disability

HAVING CEREBRAL PALSY FROM BIRTH, my initial intention when starting Counselling with Chrissie was to work with people living with visible and non-visible disabilities. My blog explains why this didn't happen.

Disability in the mainstream

The inspiration for this blog came from a conversation I had with a friend / fellow colleague regarding how to connect with people with disabilities in the mainstream. She was both shocked and surprised when I explained to her that there are no 'groups' or services for someone like me—having a disability, living independently and / or works. This left us questioning why... Why has disability been 'normalised' so much that it is deemed not necessary to provide support for the 14.6 million people with disabilities in the UK?*

There seems to be a lot more services for people that are more severely disabled, but these again are becoming limited and are heavily reliant on volunteers. I think volunteering is valuable, I have volunteered for both Cruse Bereavement Care and Mosaic Disability Services for over three years, but it does concern me how dependant we as a nation are on volunteers caring for our people who are disabled or have mental health issues.

How do you / I then connect or network with people with disabilities in the mainstream? A lot of existing help seems to be managed by the government. The hoops and red tape you have to go through with them leaves me

---

* Sourced from Scope UK, available at: https://www.scope.org.uk/media/disability-facts-figures/

asking if it is worth the effort, or what could be achieved?

A big disability organisation / charity announced they had linked up with a leading media company to start a 'Work with Me' scheme in 2015 in which they hoped to get 3 million disabled people back into work by 2020. 'Great,' I thought, 'I'd love to be part of that!' I believe that people's mental barriers, such as previous experiences of discrimination at work due to their disabilities, is what is truly keeping some people from re-entering the workplace; work with my past clients has confirmed this to be true. My ideal would be to work alongside other agencies such as Department of Work and Pensions (DWP) to enable these people to get back into work and maintain 'happy' employment.

I also contacted a nationwide scheme which helps people with disabilities that have been unemployed for two years or more to find work; concentrating on their well-being as well as finding them work. Once again, my previous experiences would be of great value here.

On both occasions I was informed I was more than welcome to help on a voluntary basis but that there were no paid roles. What does this say about the way we view those with disabilities and mental health difficulties?

However, that's not to say I haven't worked within this area. On the contrary, I have supported many clients who come to therapy with issues relating to disabilities, most of which are invisible, such as isolation—finding new friends and relationship difficulties—in both personal life and in the workplace. Many other clients have come to therapy for other reasons but have also used the time to explore their disabilities—due to wanting to be medically diagnosed—so they have a much clearer understanding of who they are and can accept themselves, realising they are not messed up, lazy, or thick. The autism spectrum is a good example of this as it can take many years for professionals to even recognise the symptoms, then longer still to be diagnosed on the NHS. If this happens after your education stage, getting support and adjustments in the workplace can be challenging but luckily, things are improving.

Letter from Kayley

Kayley came to therapy to explore why she felt so different from everyone else.

> *Over my time working with Chrissie, we challenged my beliefs around myself. I had always carried this feeling that there was something wrong with me. I thought differently to other people, I approached tasks in a different way, and I dealt with problems from different angles. It hit a point where this became a problem for me and I'd always believed this was something within me that I needed to*

fight against and overcome, to become like everyone else.

Then I started exploring the possibility that I was neurodiverse and had ADHD. As a child and into adulthood, I was often perceived by others as lazy, forgetful, idle, over enthusiastic, too sensitive and that I talked too much. This left me feeling like a burden to the people I loved and cared about, causing me a lot of internal pain and upset as I tried to fight against who I was. I developed a fear around making sure other people are okay with me, and that I'm not doing anything to upset them.

The acceptance that Chrissie gave me in the therapy room was an experience I'd not had before. There wasn't any conditions placed on the acceptance, so I was free to question myself and the labels that had been put on me by others. This safety was crucial to my journey.

Being able to explore myself and my

> *experiences and come to an understanding that I want to accept myself, allowed me to explore the idea that maybe there was nothing wrong with me as a person, that there might be something else going on with how I experience the world around me.*
>
> *This gave me the confidence to take my experiences to my doctor and the people close to me, to begin looking at whether I had ADHD. The journey is still ongoing as COVID-19 has lengthened the waiting lists to be assessed, but while I am waiting, I feel I'm in a better place, to just be me and use the ideas from therapy to help me with my everyday tasks.*

Discrimination in the workplace around disability is still evident—that is for those with disabilities who find employment to start with, as many don't. It can be mentally and emotionally damaging leaving you with no confidence and no or little self-esteem.

Letter from Joy

Joy's time in therapy helped her accept herself and her disability.

> *I initially sought out counselling to explore my negative experiences at work around disability discrimination. I had a very difficult relationship with my manager at the time, and I felt constantly targeted and put upon because I was unable to engage with work in the same way as an able-bodied person due to my disability being invisible.*
>
> *As we explored the here and now in my experiences of bullying at work, it was obvious that it brought up my past experiences of being bullied from when I was a child. There was one session in particular that really stood out to me and helped me realise that I'd been stuck in a repeating cycle. I was recounting something that had happened at work and Chrissie told me, "it feels like we've been here before."*

That became a lightbulb moment for me, and snapped me out of the circle I'd been running around in.

Chrissie introduced me to the 'Rewind Technique', where we spoke about my traumatic experiences and then recounted it in reverse. Every time I recalled this experience it followed the same pattern and I felt very stuck within it, and unable to move forward. By using the Rewind Technique and working through it backwards, I was able to look at the whole experience from a different point of view. It pulled me out of the patterns I'd been experiencing for over 15 years and gave me space to separate myself now, from myself at the time.

By doing this I was able to move on from those experiences. I was able to apply what I'd learnt from this, to my current experiences at work, and ultimately move away from being a victim to being someone who

> *is self-aware and has control of their own experiences. After doing this work, I could look at myself with more forgiveness and kindness. I accepted that my body is the way it is, that it isn't my fault, and that I am not broken or damaged. Moving forward with these new beliefs allows me to stand up for myself and my needs, and plan the life I truly wanted.*

The Rewind Technique is used to support someone who has lived a traumatic experience. They normally relive this in the same way every time they think or talk about it—like they are watching a movie over and over again. When using this technique I ask clients to tell me the experience backwards, from the end of the experience to the beginning. When doing this with a trained professional who can interject at the right time, the thoughts are remembered differently and therefore reframed in the mind in a less traumatic way.

Pause for Thought

Do you relate to what you have just read?
What were your reactions?
Have you experienced this?
Did you act against your perpetrators?
How did you rebuild your life?

Your notes:

Your notes:

10

Young Adults and Therapy

Therapy and young people

YOU SPEND THE FIRST 17 years of your life waiting to become an adult, hoping, dreaming, wishing and planning for what it's going to be like. Then the big day happens and for some, the reality does not meet your expectations. Issues that have been overlooked which manifested during childhood now decide to raise their ugly heads. As you are no longer under the Children & Young People (C&YP) criteria, getting professional help now takes months, sometimes years!

If you hadn't been shown how to cope during childhood, you will now have low resilience and become easily frustrated by everyday life events, such as college, university, work demands, relationships, problems communicating with people (not via technology), bereavement, money worries, demands on your time, being recognised as an adult by your family.

Where do you go for help? Who can you trust? How do you get a life you want?

You struggled throughout your teen years and before you know it, you are either in higher education, university, or working for minimal pay. Possibly, you want to leave home or have left home for university and now live in a city with people you don't really know. You are wanting to fit in but you don't really understanding why you are finding everything a lot harder than you expected it to be.

Were these your choices? Were you advised or told what to do by your mum or dad? Did your exam results dictate where you have ended up? Is this what you want? If so, how are you going to get through? Are you going to live the life you have ended up with but may not have chosen? Or are you going to decide to go for what you really want? How will you achieve this?

I have supported many young people working through these issues; many now live the lives they wanted and others have learned to accept and enjoy what they have.

Letter from Layla

Layla wanted to share her time with me in her own words:

> *My therapy journey began when I started to experience mental turmoil at 20-years-old, that doctors clinically diagnosed as anxiety and depression during my time at university.*
>
> *I had hopes that therapy would help me become the person I wished to be—a young woman who does not get affected by the reality of life.*

This was not the case.

You see, as a young adult who has struggled with social and family expectations, low self-esteem, relationship issues, caring what others thought of me and body image issues since my teenage years, I realised it was me vs the 'critical me'. It was the part of me that I had unconsciously developed to protect myself since my childhood.

The rise of social media since the 2010s and an Asian family's opinion and cultural opinions of what is considered as a 'sexy' body in a young woman has created a lot of dissatisfaction in how I looked at myself, causing a lot of negative impact in my self-esteem.

After sessions and sessions, I questioned myself: is there really something wrong with my body? If I didn't have the body society perceives as perfect, does that mean I'm unworthy? Chrissie has helped me realise the cause of my body image issues had a lot deeper cause than simply comparing myself to social media, per se. All I could say personally, is that I was not aware of that. I thought I wasn't good enough for my family.

There was work for me to do in between sessions, for me to look deeper at my thoughts. What was really behind my thinking? What were my true needs and wants? Was I fulfilling my needs, or other peoples'? Learning about wants and needs helps me identify what is triggering my emotional responses.

By digging deeper into my mind, and untangling all the knots around my brain with Chrissie's help, I realised why I am the way I am right now. Then through the understanding, I achieved; I then became empowered to change the way I think for myself and ONLY for myself.

Although, sometimes I try to improve my way of thinking and develop myself for the good, there is something that stops me. I didn't understand what was going on.

I then go back to Chrissie and discuss this deeper. By the time I finish the session, I have never failed to find the cause, and by finding it, I can create understanding in a way that empowers me to make the changes that I want.

Have you ever had that horrible boss / teacher / anyone above you in title who made you feel incompetent? Who made you start doubting yourself due to your low confidence? The 'old' me thought there was something wrong with me—caring what others thought of me—yet the 'new' me realises the boss is just an 'arsehole', so I decided to give back the 'shit' that had nothing to do with me. I couldn't change my boss but I could change me.

As I dealt with someone in a higher position, I realised, with Chrissie's help, that this was due to unsolved issues with authority figures. Being due to the way I internalised unjustified disciplinary actions from my dad as a child. Knowing this, I can be strong enough to set my boundaries and stand up for myself when facing 'injustice' situations.

I know life will always throw small or large challenges at me. I cannot control my external circumstances, however, what I can control is how I can cope with these circumstance. Through therapy, I have learned skills overtime that I call 'tools', which I store in a 'toolbox'. As life happens, I would go back to the toolbox and see what I can use to cope.

Therapy isn't always sunshine and roses. Sometimes, what goes on in my life—things that cause me stress—could be something that brings me to my reality. I will be called out on this; Chrissie will challenge my thinking and enable me to see what the real issues are. Like when I get involved in family dramas—which get me down—yet the real issue was that I was lonely and needed connection of any kind, even negative connection. By the time I finish my sessions with Chrissie, I will tell myself, "yes that's true, I did bring that on myself." I realised I was creating my own stress by getting over involved and affected by outcomes. I realised I need to change this behaviour.'

I did have sessions where I felt embarrassed, got upset, and cried, but however I was feeling, it is ok. That's part of therapy.

You might find that your therapist was that parent you are able to talk to, that older sister who guides you in life as you are similar, who has more experience—which is my case—that teacher who coaches you in certain aspects of your life... you never know. Chrissie became the big sister I wanted but never had, all within the boundaries we agreed.

As time progressed, I realised I was becoming that empowered person, that person I wished I was when all those life challenges from the past were confronting me. I no longer have issues with my body image. My self-esteem and confidence have grown beyond anything I expected, or dared imagine.

When we used the 'Miracle Dream Technique', which focuses on your ideal life, I realised what I wanted wasn't completely out of reach. I loved that session!

Starting and continuing therapy over a three-year period, has been the best decision I could've ever made, having no other support system in my life as a young adult growing up, self-exploring and forming my identity.

I have gone from considering leaving university in my first year, to graduating, finding work I love, and living away from my unsupportive family. As I now wait to become a mum, I hope to pass on what I have learned from Chrissie to my child and continue to use my newfound knowledge in the years to come. Hopefully preventing my child from experiencing the issues that were holding me back.

If you would like support for issues similar to these, please contact me at:

counsellingwithchrissie.co.uk
chrissiehenson@hotmail.com

Pause for Thought

Are you a young adult who is struggling with the issues highlighted in this chapter?
What support do you have?
Would you like to choose a different outcome?

Your notes:

Your notes:

11

Rejection and Therapy

Rejection in childhood

Having an emotionally absent mother affects you as a child and as an adult.

THE LACK OF PHYSICAL COMFORT and nurturing leaves you feeling unsafe in the world and unable to cope when things aren't going right. It's because you haven't been shown how to make yourself feel better as a child, so haven't got the skills to self-sooth as an adult.

As you grow up and start forming relationships, you may look for that 'parent figure' in friends, partners, therapists and even bosses. Seeking their love and approval can lead to over pleasing—filling another person's wants and needs and not your own.

Some mothers go further with controlling

behaviour, not only denying you their love, but actively destroying the love and happiness you find somewhere else. They put the other people in your life down, telling you that you are not wanted or good enough. After hearing this repeatedly for years, you start to believe it. You develop a lack of self-worth and have low confidence, as you are obviously 'unloveable' if your mum couldn't love you. Eventually you stop thinking that someone could love you for you.

If you haven't resolved the issues of being rejected or treated as being unloveable, you may end up entering other relationships where the outcome is detrimental. For example: even when you find someone to have a 'healthy' relationship with, it may not last. It starts off being two-way, they care about your dreams, wishes, things that make you happy. However, that slowly changes, and you give more to still be wanted, fulfilling their dreams, wishes and sometimes becoming the one doing all the running around after them. To not be abandoned again. Even though everything inside you is saying you are 'being used' or 'put on' to meet their conditions of worth. You tell yourself this is still better than being alone, they do love you it's just...

You have put yourself in the situation to create a similar outcome, not because it makes you happy, but because it is familiar to you.

Letter from Jenny

Whilst I was at university I started to struggle getting out of bed, I just couldn't face the day or people. It was a debilitating type of sadness that I could not explain. I was told by my mum to get myself checked at the doctors, as she didn't have time to deal with this. She never has time for me. As a child we lived with my nan after Nan discovered Mum would leave me home alone at aged three so she could see her friends or to go to work, Dad had left when I was two.

I never expected I would struggle with my mental health so was shocked by how bad my mental health had gotten so quickly. I spoke to the doctor and was diagnosed with anxiety and depression. I chose private therapy as I wanted help quickly, I feel very lucky to have found Chrissie the first time I searched online for a therapist; we got on well from my first session.

We discussed my struggles socially and academically, as I didn't find university life easy, constantly questioning my relationships with other people, especially when it came to trusting them or feeling included. In therapy I learned that my limits of what I would accept and give were weak around people. I needed to feel liked by everyone, and not be rejected. I would never say what I wanted or how

I felt. I could describe these as 'warm up' sessions. Thinking about it, I could say Chrissie and I were exploring the first few layers of my issues before I got into the 'core' of the work.

After I left university, I noticed a decline in my mental health again after returning home to live with mum. I decided to continue therapy and with Chrissie's help, I realised the problem was deeply rooted. The relationship I had with Mum would be... let's say... one of the biggest causes of my poor mental health. Her unhelpful behaviour and the way she spoke to me was detrimental. She would call me selfish for wanting to move out and start my life outside the area since I had found my dream job as a graduate. She had other plans and wanted us—rather me—to buy us a house. Not for us to live together, but so she had a rent-free place to live. My dreams didn't matter. Mum's opinions and feelings were always valid, to her, but mine weren't. I started to believe I was being selfish, and I became unhappy—I didn't know why.

I came to realise with Chrissie's help that this was her way to get what she wanted, by having 'tantrums' and putting me down, being critical and cold towards me, never being there when I needed her, leaving me feeling rejected. She had done this all my life; I don't remember being hugged or told I was loved as a child. I did not know this was known as narcissistic behaviour.

I realised I always looked at what I consider as negative traits of myself, but I never paid attention to my positives. I came to understand this was because Mum always emphasised my negatives but never embraced my positives?

Throughout my therapy, I realised I had to be the one who changed, set boundaries of what I will and won't accept and put my needs and wants first. I noticed Mum's behaviour towards me has also changed as she realises she can't upset me anymore. The boundaries I built through therapy helped me stop hurting.

I still long for that mum I wanted and needed, and not to be rejected by her, but with the help of therapy I came to realise that 'I' can be the mum I need and want; I can look after me and live a happy life.

Pause for Thought

Can you identify with what you have just read?
Is there someone in your life that you feel your relationship with just isn't right?
How would you like to relate to others?

Your notes:

Your notes:

12

Men and Therapy

Male rape

> As a man you think, rape doesn't happen to a man. It couldn't happen as men were perpetrators not prey. It couldn't happen to a man and the realisation when it does, confounds all sensibilities.
>
> I looked in the mirror, a shattered mirror and I saw so many broken reflections of myself. I realised I was the victim of rape. Another man had complete control and power over me and I could not speak out. I kept looking at those broken reflections of myself and realised my only way out was to speak out. Therapy saved me from my destruction.
>
> Billy

Billy, 48, came for therapy to get an understanding of why he keeps attracting the same kind of men who use and abuse him.

The oldest of four boys, his upbringing was physically abusive. His mum would beat the boys for anything she deemed as bad behaviour, then would inform their father when he returned home from work. He was a strict man and would instruct them to lower their pants, then spank them with his belt, often for things they had been accused of and not done. The younger brothers would blame Billy for their bad behaviours to avoid punishment themselves, resulting in extra beatings for Billy.

Knowing what was happening in the family home and knowing Billy wouldn't tell his parents what was happening, at aged 12, Billy was raped by his 19 year old cousin.

Years later and after numerous relationships that were physically or mentally abusive, Billy met John. Their relationship was amazing, John cooked lovely meals, showered him with gifts and they spent every waking moment together. Billy thought he had finally met someone, he could trust, love and be loved by.

Gradually, John started finding fault with little things Billy did, like putting a cup in the wrong kitchen cupboard, the clothes he wore or how he styled his hair. John would cause an argument if Billy arranged to see his friends or people from work for a drink or a meal, often texting 20–30 times an hour, asking where he was and when he would be home. This went on until Billy felt it wasn't worth the hassle and decided to stay home instead, thinking this would please John, but it actually made things a lot worse.

Knowing Billy had no one to tell, John's coercive behaviour intensified, ordering Billy to wear just his underwear around the house, even when his friends were there, telling them he was just too lazy to get dressed. After months of this treatment, Billy had no confidence and very low self-esteem. John's behaviour became worse, he started coming home with friends and ordered Billy to allow them to rape him, sometimes it was more than one man, this and the mind games went on for months.

Then one day, Billy was home alone on the computer, and found a group that helped men escape abusive relationships, having enough time to message the group, he was helped to escape. He reported John to the police and got placed in a safehouse miles away from where they lived.

During therapy, Billy explored the abuse from his parents, acknowledging this was his past and didn't have to be his present or future. He explored the treatment he had endured by John and various other men throughout his adult life. Billy came to realise he had been attracting different versions of his father and cousin within his relationships and believed that this was what he deserved and there was nothing better out there for him. In therapy terms, this is known as a core belief and is something you truly believe to be real, even if there is evidence stating the opposite view. I often describe this being like words in a stick of rock. You believe so strongly, it's like it runs through the middle of you; it can take a lot of work to change or undo. Working together for months we slowly unpicked these beliefs.

Billy was so engulfed in helping others that he lost any sense of being vulnerable to further abuses. He'd been abused as a child and thought it couldn't happen again as an adult. He was charmed, seduced, then coerced and pushed into a fully vulnerable state of being. He didn't recognise that he was being groomed in adulthood until he realised he was being raped and felt trapped. He was a broken man being raped repeatedly and feeling his life was over. Feeling that he had to live like that, suffer like that, with no way out until he broke his own silence and sought help. Once he spoke out his transition from the horrific ordeal, he'd lived under, the change was swift. Billy cannot be ashamed of what he accepted as a new reality. Billy's confidence, self-esteem, and outlook on life increased. He moved house, changed his job, and found new friends, and is now living a very happy life.

For others who have experienced male rape, silence is never the answer. Speaking out, seeking help is. Billy is the living proof of that. I saw Billy about a year after therapy had ended, he was a different man to the one I had first met. I was happy to know that in a very small way, I was part of what made that change happen. I'll leave this chapter with his words.

> *I was very dubious about trying a new therapy. I didn't know what I needed but I had reached a point that I knew I was almost eating myself from the inside and there was so little left in me. I had*

reached true desperation. I needed help more than I ever had before because my mind was flipping around so fast that I had no reason to exist anymore and I was falling to pieces. I felt I could destroy my life completely and no one would ever care, but then I met Chrissie, my therapist, and decided I had to talk. Talk, talk and talk. She listened and guided me, heard all of my thoughts flooding out, asking for help. If it wasn't for the therapy I had through her then I wouldn't be writing these words. She listened and guided me away from the brink of complete self-destruction.

Pause for Thought

There is a lot of detail regarding male rape, abuse, grooming and controlling behaviour in this chapter please give yourself time to reflect on your feelings.

Your notes:

Your notes:

Summary

My hope for anyone reading this book, who previously had fears or concerns about attending therapy, now feels it will be a safe place for them to address their issues.

For those experiencing or have experienced the topics highlighted in this book, I hope you will feel there IS another way and will find the strength needed to seek help themselves.

I hope that I have inspired anyone who has ever been told they couldn't do something because of their disability, gender, age, sexuality, race or any other reason and feel they CAN do whatever it is they are being told they can't and never stop trying, hoping and dreaming for better things.

Any Other Notes

Do you have any other thoughts from reading this book that you would like to write down? Please use this space for those thoughts.

Your notes:

Your notes:

About the Author

Chrissie Henson

My professional background has always included caring for, or supporting, other people in some way. After leaving college I worked with children under five then moved to under 12's in a kids club. I have had roles in customer services, sales, and project management, working mainly for big companies.

After being made redundant in 2013, I took the opportunity to return to education and training as a person-centred therapist, which took three years to complete and included placements with charities for bereaved adults and Mosaic who support people living with disabilities.

Having a physical disability since birth myself, Mosaic Disability Services is somewhere I am passionate about, so I continued to volunteer there for a year after I qualified. Then I decided if I was going to make therapy my future career, it was now or never.

In 2018 I founded Counselling with Chrissie, my private practise. I initially started off being an associate in a team of therapists, whilst also working at Leicester University as a counsellor.

After two years, I rented a room on my own, then due to COVID-19, I moved my practise to my home and online, where I still work today. When clients have their face-to-face sessions, they are often joined by Fiz, my current therapy dog (pictured), he normally finds a comfortable space to lie, but will go to clients if they become upset, or they simply just want a cuddle with him. Clients are informed he is present beforehand and have the option to say they prefer not to have him in the therapy room at all.

I have recently expanded to offer courses called 'Bite Size Therapy', for those people who either want to work on their issues in private or want to undertake personal development.

I have experienced therapy, both as a therapist and as a client, and know the personal benefits and the growth I gained from having therapy. Which is one of the reasons I continue my work to support other people to gain the life they want and deserve.

Other Services by the Author

1-2-1 Therapy

Bite Size Therapy – courses and worksheets that you can work on at your own pace at home.

For more information please see my website: counsellingwithchrissie.co.uk

You can book a FREE 15-minute session to discuss which course best suits your needs.

Facebook: Counselling with Chrissie Henson page, for tips on mental health and self-care

Facebook Group: University Overwhelm Coach, for tips on mental health and self-care for university students and post-graduates

Printed in Great Britain
by Amazon